Gone Forever!
Stegosaurus

Rupert Matthews

Heinemann Library
Chicago, Illinois

Customer Service 888-454-2279
Visit our website at www.heinemannlibrary.com

Designed by Ron Kamen and Paul Davies and Associates
Illustrations by James Field of Simon Girling and Associates
Photo Research by Rebecca Sodergren and Ginny Stroud-Lewis
Originated by Ambassador Litho Ltd.
Printed and bound in China by South China Printing Company

07 06 05 04
10 9 8 7 6 5 4 3 2

Library of Congress Cataloging-in-Publication Data
Matthews, Rupert.
  Stegosaurus / Rupert Matthews.
     p. cm. -- (Gone forever!)
Summary: Describes what has been learned about the physical features,
behavior, and surroundings of the long-extinct stegosaurus.
Includes bibliographical references and index.
  ISBN 1-4034-3658-4 (hardcover) -- ISBN 1-4034-3669-X (pbk.)
  1. Stegosaurus--Juvenile literature. [1. Stegosaurus. 2. Dinosaurs.]
I. Title.
  QE862.O65M36 2003
  567.915'3--dc22

                              2003012298

Acknowledgments
The author and publishers are grateful to the following for permission to reproduce copyright material: p. 16 Paul A. Souders/Corbis; p. 24 Richard Cummins/Corbis; pp. 6, 8, 12, 14, 18, 20, 22 Geoscience Features; pp. 4, 10 Natural History Museum, London; p. 26 Senekenberg Nature Museum/DK.
Cover photograph reproduced with permission of Geoscience Features.

Special thanks to Dr. Peter Makovicky of the Chicago Field Museum for his review of this book.

Some words are shown in bold, **like this.** You can find out what they mean by looking in the glossary.

Contents

Gone Forever!

Sometimes all the animals of a certain type die. This means that the animal has become **extinct.** Scientists called **paleontologists** study the **fossils** of these animals. They find out about the animal and how it lived.

Stegosaurus

Brachiosaurus

The **dinosaur** called Stegosaurus is an extinct
animal. It lived about 150 million years ago in North
America. It ate plants. All the other dinosaurs that
lived at this time have also become extinct.

Stegosaurus's Home

Geologists are scientists who study rocks. They have looked at the rocks where **fossils** of Stegosaurus have been found. These rocks can tell us many things about the place where Stegosaurus lived.

Stegosaurus lived in a wide, flat land. Huge rivers flowed across the land. The weather was warm and often damp. Wet **marsh** covered some areas, but trees grew on the drier land.

7

Plants

The rocks that have Stegosaurus **fossils** in them also have the fossils of plants. **Fir** trees, **monkey-puzzle** trees, and **gingko** trees all grew at the time of Stegosaurus. Plants like these still grow today.

fossil of leaves from a gingko tree

8

cycadeoid gingko pine tree

horsetail fern

During the time of Stegosaurus, there were many more **ferns** and **horsetails** than there are today. They grew much larger than the ones alive now. Some plants of that time are now **extinct.** One of these was the **cycadeoid.** The cycadeoid had a short, fat trunk topped by a clump of leaves.

9

Living with Stegosaurus

Paleontologists have found **fossils** of small animals in the same rocks where Stegosaurus fossils have been found. This shows that these animals lived at the same time as Stegosaurus. One of these fossils was a frog. It looked like the fossil frog shown here.

fossil of a frog

10

Many other small animals lived with Stegosaurus. **Insects, newts,** and **lizards** crawled along the ground. **Mammals** that looked like **shrews** hunted insects.

cockroach

shrewlike mammal

lizard

frog

newt

What Was Stegosaurus?

By studying **fossils, paleontologists** can tell what an animal looked like and how it lived. They have studied Stegosaurus fossils. For example, they know that Stegosaurus ate plants.

head

tail

12

Stegosaurus was about as long as two station wagons parked end to end. Stegosaurus had a very small head. Its brain was about the size of a walnut. It was probably not very smart!

Baby Stegosaurus

Scientists have found **fossils** of **dinosaur** eggs. However, no Stegosaurus eggs have been found. Perhaps Stegosaurus partly buried its eggs in the ground, like the eggs below.

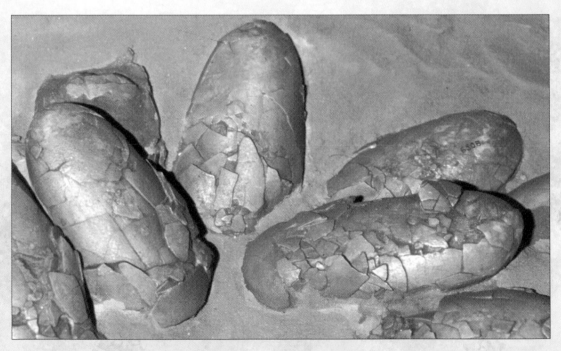

fossils of eggs belonging to Oviraptor

No fossils of baby Stegosauruses have been found. When baby Stegosauruses **hatched,** perhaps they dug themselves out of the ground. Then they might have hidden among the plants that grew on the forest floor. There they would have been safer from meat-eating dinosaurs.

Reaching for Food

Stegosaurus's front legs were much shorter than its back legs. This means that Stegosaurus held its head close to the ground. It could crouch so that its head could reach down to the ground.

Paleontologists think that Stegosaurus ate
plants that grew about as high as your shoulder.
The most common plants of that size were **ferns.**
Stegosaurus probably ate ferns.

Stegosaurus's Dinner

Stegosaurus **fossils** show that this **dinosaur** had small teeth. Its jaws were also small. The **muscles** that moved the jaws were very weak. This meant that Stegosaurus could not chew tough plants very well.

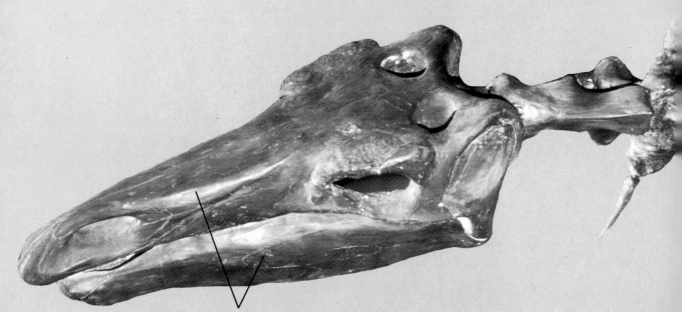

Stegosaurus jaws

Scientists think that Stegosaurus bit off pieces of
ferns. It swallowed them without chewing. The
ferns were **digested** in the stomach for a long
time. This meant that Stegosaurus needed to have
a huge stomach.

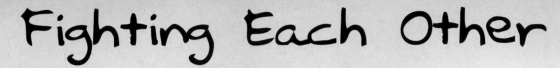

Fighting Each Other

Stegosaurus had large plates along its back that stuck straight up. These plates were made of bone covered with skin. Scientists believe that Stegosaurus might have been able to change the color of its skin.

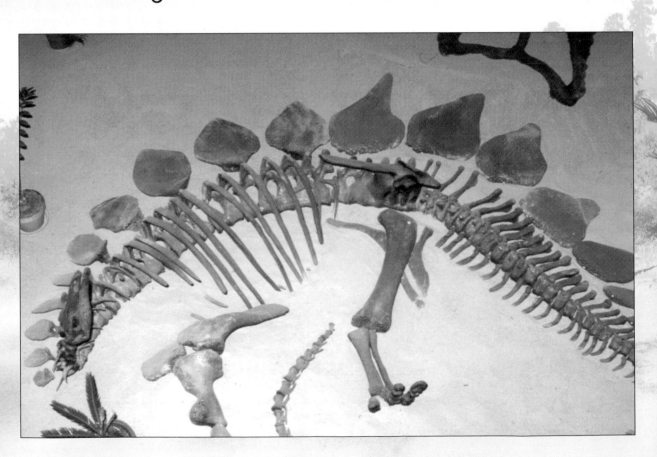

Sometimes two Stegosauruses would want to eat in the same area. Perhaps the **dinosaurs** used their plates and changed color to make themselves look scary and powerful. The one that put on the best show would scare the other Stegosaurus away.

Keeping Warm

Fossils of Stegosaurus's back plates are covered with grooves and ridges. These grooves show that the plates had many **blood vessels** that carried blood to them.

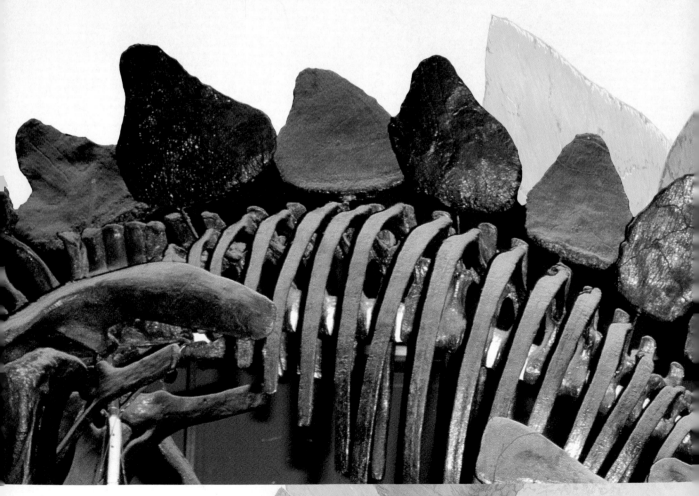

Some scientists think that the plates helped warm up Stegosaurus's body. The plates might have soaked up warmth from the sun. Or maybe the plates helped cool Stegosaurus down. The blood vessels in the plates could have carried heat from its body.

Danger!

A **dinosaur** called
Allosaurus lived at
the same time as
Stegosaurus. Allosaurus
was a large **predator.**
It hunted Stegosaurus
for food.

24

Paleontologists think Allosaurus might have hidden among trees. It dashed out to jump on any Stegosaurus that came close. Allosaurus could kill Stegosaurus using its long claws and sharp teeth.

25

Fighting Back

Stegosaurus **fossils** show that it had four large spikes on the end of its tail. These spikes were made of bone and were very sharp.

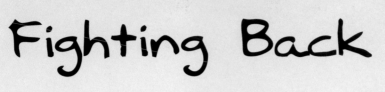

Paleontologists think that Stegosaurus could use its spikes to fight off meat-eating **dinosaurs.** Stegosaurus would whip its tail from side to side. To keep from being hurt, an Allosaurus might leave a Stegosaurus alone.

27

Where Did Stegosaurus Live?

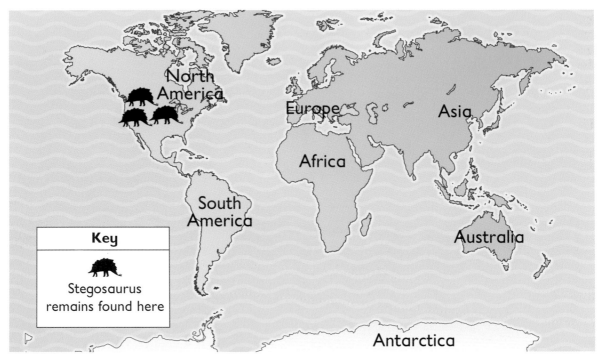

Key

Stegosaurus remains found here

Paleontologists have found Stegosaurus **fossils** in North America. They have found fossils of **dinosaurs** like Stegosaurus in Africa, China, and Europe.

When Did Stegosaurus Live?

Stegosaurus lived on Earth in the Age of the Dinosaurs. Scientists call this time the Mesozoic Era. Stegosaurus lived between 150 and 140 million years ago. This was at the end of what paleontologists call the Jurassic Period.

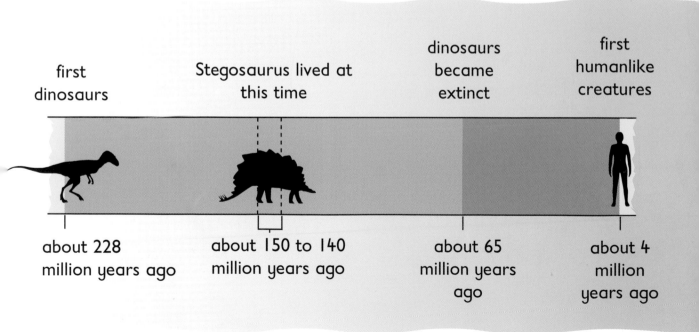

first dinosaurs	Stegosaurus lived at this time	dinosaurs became extinct	first humanlike creatures
about 228 million years ago	about 150 to 140 million years ago	about 65 million years ago	about 4 million years ago

Fact File

Stegosaurus	
Length:	up to 30 feet (9 meters)
Height:	up to 16 feet (5 meters)
Weight:	4,400 pounds (2,000 kilograms)
Time:	Late Jurassic Period, about 150 to 140 million years ago
Place:	North America

How to Say It

Allosaurus—al-uh-sore-us

cycadeoid—sy-kad-ee-oid

dinosaur—dine-ah-sor

Stegosaurus—steg-oh-sore-us

Glossary

blood vessel tube that carries blood around the body

cycadeoid plant that looked like a cross between a palm and a fern. They are now extinct.

digested describes the process that happens in the stomach and other body parts so that food can be used by the body for fuel

dinosaur reptile that lived on Earth between 228 and 65 million years ago. Dinosaurs are extinct.

extinct word that describes plants and animals that once lived on Earth but have all died out

fern green plant with large feathery leaves and no flowers

fir tree that keeps its leaves all year. The leaves are skinny and always green.

fossil remains of a plant or animal, usually found in rocks

geologist scientist who studies rocks

gingko type of tree with fan-shaped leaves

hatch break out of an egg

horsetail type of plant with a straight stem and spiky leaves

insect small animal with a hard outer covering and six legs

lizard small reptile with four legs and usually a long tail

mammal animal with hair or fur. Mammals give birth to live young and feed them on milk from the mother's body.

marsh land that is partly covered by water

monkey-puzzle type of tree with spiked branches

muscle part of an animal's body that makes it move

newt small animal with four legs that lives both in and out of water

paleontologist scientist who studies fossils. Paleontologists discover things about extinct animals, such as dinosaurs.

predator animal that hunts and eats other animals

shrew type of small mammal with a long nose

31

More Books to Read

Cohen, Daniel. *Stegosaurus and Other Jurassic Plant-Eaters*. Mankato, Minn.: Capstone Press, 1996.

Rodriguez, K. S. *Stegosaurus*. Chicago: Raintree, 2000.

Wilkes, Angela. *Big Book of Dinosaurs*. New York: Dorling Kindersley Publishing, 2001.

Index